An Ordinance Organizing

and Establishing

Patrols for the

Police of Slaves

in the Parish of St. Landry

By Saint Landry Parish

Originally published
1863

AN ORDINANCE To organize and establish Patrols for the Police of Slaves in the Parish of St. Landry.

Article 1st. The Police Jury of the Parish of St. Landry ordains as follows:

Art. 2d. Every free white male person, having attained the age of 16 years and not above the age of 60 years, who shall reside in the State of Louisiana and Parish of St. Landry, shall be bound to do patrol duty within the limits of the Patrol District in which he resides, or in any District in which he may be ordered. —

Art. 3d. It shall be the duty of the Parish Superintendent of Patrols, in

1

addition to any — other duties that may be imposed on him by existing laws:

1st. To divide the Parish into as many Patrol Districts as he may find expedient, and to change the same whenever it may be necessary.

2d. To appoint and commission in each Patrol District, a fit and proper person, as Captain of Patrol, and to fill all vacancies.

3d. To dismiss any Captain of Patrol, and to accept their resignations, and to demand and receive from any Captain of Patrol, who may leave the bounds of the District for which he was appointed, or who may resign, or who may be dismissed, or suspended, his commission as Captain of Patrol.

4th. To issue such orders, or instructions, to the Captains of Patrols, the leaders of patrol, or the patrol, relative to their respective duties, as he may deem expedient or necessary for the service.

5th. To pay attention that the Captains of Patrol perform the duties enjoined on them by law, and to cause to be prosecuted such as fail to perform any of their duties.

6th. To keep a list or roll of the persons appointed as Captains or leaders of Patrols, and the number of men under each leader, noting the dates of their several appointment, and of all changes, and to keep à copy of all orders or instructions by him issued.

7th. To form any settlement of free persons of color into a patrol District, on the petition of a majority of such persons being free holders, should he deem it expedient, and to cause all free persons of color residing in such District, between the ages of eighteen and forty-five years, to be enrolled and do duty as a patrol, in the limits of such Districts only, in the same manner and under the same responsibilities, penalties and forfeitures as the other patrols in this parish, Provided, That the patrols of free persons of color shall not patrol out of such district, or patrol on the plantations of any white person, unless specially requested in writing so to do. And also provided, That the patrols of white persons shall patrol in such district, the same as if it had net been erected into a patrol district, and the patrol of free persons of color shall at all times, and under every circumstance, be obedient and subordinate to all Captains, leaders, or patrols of white persons when on duty.

8th. To file with the Clerk of the Police Jury of this parish the boundaries of the patrol district made by him, as well as all the changes thereof, To deliver to the said Clerk a certified list of the Captains and leaders of patrol, with the number of the district or ward for which they have been appointed, whenever thereunto requested by the said Clerk or the Police Jury of the parish, and notifying to said Clerk all changes in any appointment.

9th. To report to the Police Jury of this Parish at every regular meeting, the manner in which the laws relative to the patrols have been executed, and suggesting such alterations in, or amendments to said laws as experience may have shown to be necessary or proper.

10th. To counsel and give advice to all Captains and leaders of patrol, whenever requested, relative to the duties enjoined on them by law, and to aid and assist them in making out their reports and returns, by furnishing them with blank forms therefor, and showing the manner in which they are to be filled in.

11th. At the expense of the parish, to cause all such books, blanks, papers, laws, &c., to be printed, as may be deemed necessary for the information and government of the patrols.

Art. 4th. In case the said parish Superintendent should at any time be unable to act, or should resign, or be dismissed, or be absent, his duties will be performed by the President of the

Police Jury until the Superintendent is able to resume his duties, or a person is appointed in his place as the case may be.

Art. 5th. The persons to be appointed as Captains of patrol shall be bound to serve two years in every five years, but may each retain his commission, and act under the same until he resigns, or is superseded by the parish Superintendent, and any person who refuses to serve as Captain of patrol, shall forfeit and pay a fine of not less than twenty-five dollars, nor more than five hundred dollars.

Art. 6th. It shall be the duty of every person appointed a Captain of patrol—

1st. To cause to be made, and always to keep, a list or roll of all persons in his district subject to patrol duty, and to cause to be enrolled, from time to time, every person so liable, who shall arrive at the age of sixteen years, or who shall come to reside in his district, which list or roll he shall keep in a book, agreeably to the form to be furnished by the Superintendent of patrol and deliver the same, and all books and papers, belonging to the office of Captain of patrol, to his successor in office, or to the said Superintendent.

2d. He shall divide the persons so enrolled into such number of squads as he may deem necessary, in such manner that there shall not be less than three persons to each squad, to each of which squads he shall appoint a fit person as leader.

3rd. He shall cause patrols to be made in his District, or out of it, if relieved by the Superintendent, in such manner that his whole district — shall be patrolled at least once in every week, and as much oftener as he may deem it expedient.

4th. He shall pay attention that all patrols ordered take place, and make return of all delinquent leaders of Patrol, or members of a Patrol to any Justice of the Peace in the Parish, within twenty-four hours after any delinquency shall have come to his knowledge.

5th. To take (at such time as he may deem it expedient,) command of any squad or squads that may be either out, or that he may order out, and patrol therewith, in which case he shall report to the Superintendent of patrol, stating — fully the reasons that induced him to assume the command.

6th. To make returns of the state of his district to the Superintendent of patrol, in the manner required, and agreeably to the forms to be furnished on the first day of March, June, September and December in every year. He shall deliver to each leader of patrol, a commission of his appointment, stating therein the number of his squad, and endorsing thereon the names of the leaders of patrols in the district, and the names of the persons composing his squad, which will be sufficient authority for him to command such persons to patrol.

7th. To have power-to dismiss any leader of patrol, accept their resignations, and fill all vacancies that may occur, and

8th. To be bound to obey all orders, or instructions, issued by the parish Superintendent of patrols.

9th. Any Captain of patrol who shall fail to perform any of the duties imposed on him by this section, shall forfeit and pay a fine not less than ten dollars nor more than fifty dollars.

Art. 7th. The persons to be appointed as leaders of patrol shall be freeholders, and be at least twenty-one years of age, and shall, be bound to serve one year in every two years. And the said leaders of patrol shall be bound and it shall be their duty—

1st. To attend personally, and lead every patrol that may be ordered.

2d. To obey all orders issued by their Captain, or the parish Superintendent.

3d. To give, or cause to be given, to every person composing à patrol, verbal or written notice of the time and place of the meeting of patrol.

4th. To inform the Captains of the names of such persons as they may know are not enrolled.

5th. To see that each person under their orders attend and do their duty.

6th. To report to their Captain, within thirty-six hours after their patrol has gone its rounds, or sooner if necessary, the names of every delinquent in their squad, and the occurrences that may have happened, and

7th. To do and perform all such other duties as shall be enjoined on them by law.

8th. Any Leader of patrol who shall fail to perform any of the duties imposed on him by this article, shall forfeit and pay a fine not less than ten, nor more than fifty dollars, and in default of payment be imprisoned in the Parish Jail not more than twenty-four hours.

Art. 8th. The leaders of patrol when appointed, shall be numbered one, two, three, &c., and when two or more squads are, ordered out; at one time, or accidently meet, the lowest number shall command the others, and the said leaders of patrol shall have power—

1st. To call on any individual in the district for aid and assistance; or on any leader of patrol for the aid of his squad, the leader called upon to be subject to and obey the orders of the leader who makes the call.

2d. To either patrol with his whole squad or divide them into detachments, as he may deem necessary—or detach or order one or more of his squad on a particular service, when he deems it expedient.

Art. 9th. Whenever a patrol, or squad of patrol, is ordered on duty, or is on duty, or it is its turn to patrol, and the leader thereof is either absent or unable to attend, or is compelled to absent himself, the said leader shall deliver or cause to be delivered his commission to one of the patrol, being a freeholder and 21 years of age and shall be by him retained, during the tour of duty, or until the leader assumes command. The person having the commission aforesaid shall be leader of the patrol, and command the same, under the same responsibilities, penalties, and forfeitures, as if he was named in the commission as the leader of that patrol, and the members of the patrol shall be bound to obey the person in possession of the commission as aforesaid, under the penalties prescribed for disobedience of orders.

Art. 10th. It shall be the duty of every patrol, or detailment thereof to patrol within the limits of the Parish pointed out by the Captain or Superintendent, and in case of necessity within the bounds of the entire district, during the hours either of night or day, as they may be ordered, or to the leader may seem fit, to maintain tranquility in and watch over the safety of their district or limits, to arrest and detain all free persons whom they shall find committing disorders or disturbing the public peace, and all vagabonds and suspicious persons, and carry them within twelve hours thereafter, before any Justice of the Peace in the Parish enter on all plantations, to visit the negro huts, or places suspected of entertaining unlawful assemblies of slaves.

Art. 11th. Any person subject to patrol duty, who shall refuse or neglect to attend any patrol with his arms, when ordered, or to send a substitute in his place, to be accepted by the leader of the patrol, or who, having once attended, shall absent himself without the permission of the leader of patrol, or who shall be guilty of disobedience of orders, or disorderly conduct when on duty, or who shall neglect or refuse to aid and assist a patrol when required by the leader thereof, shall forfeit and pay a sum that shall not exceed fifty dollars, nor be less than ten dollars, and in default of payment be imprisoned in the Parish Jail not more than twenty-four hours.

Art. 12th. All slaves who shall be found at any unlawful assembly of slaves—all slaves who shall be found out of the plantation or place to which they belong, or where they are habitually employed, or who shall be found strolling, without the permission in writing, required by law, or some token, known to the patrol, and that may have been agreed upon with the owner, or person having such slaves in charge—all slaves having a permission or token, who shall be found out of the direct road going to or from the place they have permission to go to and from—all slaves who shall be found gambling, or looking on at others gambling, or permitting gambling in their cabin, whether such gambling be played with cards, or dice, or other things, and whether such gambling be for amusement, money or any other thing—all slaves who shall refuse to surrender to, or shall resist or break from a patrol, or shall give a false account of themselves, or their business, to a patrol, shall severally receive from the patrol a number of stripes, moderately inflicted, not to exceed fifty.

Art. 13th. All cards, dice or other things used to gamble with, and found with any slave, shall be taken and destroyed by the patrol, and all animals, arms, or other things found with a slave at any unlawful assembly of slaves, or with any slave not having the permission re. quired by law, shall be seized and taken possession of by, the patrol, and disposed of as the law directs.

Art. 14th. Any slaves who, to a patrol or a detachment of a patrol, shall refuse to surrender or shall escape from custody, or shall give a false account of him or herself, or of his or her business, shall receive not more than fifty stripes, at the discretion of the Captain of patrol, which the person having charge of such slave, shall be bound to cause to be inflicted, on the demand of the Captain of patrol, and in case of refusal or neglect, every such person shall forfeit and pay a fine of not less than twenty nor more than one hundred dollars, and in default of payment be imprisoned in the Parish Jail not more than twenty-four hours: Provided that no slave shall be stopped if sent in behalf of a sick person, but the fact shall be reported, and if found to be false, the slave shall be punished as aforesaid.

Art. 15th. The permission, in writing, to be carried by a slave, shall be in conformity with the laws of the State, and shall be in the following form, to-wit:

The bearer, (negro or mulatto) named ____, has leave to go from ____ to ____ for ____ days, (or hours,) dated

23

the same day of the delivery; which said permission shall be signed — by the owner, or with his consent, and shall only serve for the time necessary for the slave to perform the object of such permission.

Art. 16th. There shall he forfeited, and paid as a fine, not less than twenty-five dollars, nor more than one hundred dollars, and in default of payment be imprisoned not more than twenty-four hours in the Parish Jail—

1st. By whomsoever shall represent himself as a captain or as a leader, or as a member of a patrol on duty, without sufficient authority for doing so.

2d. By whoever shall, when called upon, refuse or neglect to aid and assist any patrol, or any member thereof, in the discharge of their or his duty.

3d. By whoever shall, when required, neglect or refuse to comply with any lawful order given by a captain or leader of a patrol, or given by a member of a patrol on duty.

4th. By whoever shall resist or oppose, or shall obstruct or annoy, or shall abuse or insult, or shall behave in a disrespectful manner to daily patrol, or to any captain, leader, or member of a patrol, whilst in the lawful discharge of their duty either as a patrol, or as a captain leader, or member of a patrol.

5th. By whoever, in the presence of a slave, or who, within the hearing of a slave, and knowing a slave to be either present or within hearing, shall resist, or oppose, or shall obstruct, or annoy, or shall insult or use abusive language, or shall behave in a disrespectful manner to any patrol, or squad, or detachment of a patrol, whilst acting in the lawful discharge of their duty or duties.

6th. By whoever shall take away, or drive away, any animal, or shall let out of any enclosure or other place, where it may have been put, any animal, such animal either belonging to, or being in charge of any patrol, or to any person employed by a patrol.

7th. By whoever shall take or carry say, or shall in any manner injure or destroy any animals, article or thing seized by any patrol or by any member of a patrol—or being in the care or charge of, or belonging to any patrol or any member of a patrol, or to any person employed either by a patrol or by a member of a patrol.

8th. By whoever shall neglect or refuse to admit a patrol, or any member of a patrol, on: duty, into such places under his or her control, as the leader of patrol may lawfully visit, inspect or search.

27

9th. By whoever shall be found in the cabin or house of any slave or slaves, and not being the owner, or having the charge of any such slave or slaves.

10th. By whoever shall intentionally give to the Chief Captain of Patrol, of to a captain, leader, or a member of patrol, any false information either relative to the patrol, or that may cause a patrol to be ordered out, or that may change the route of a patrol on duty, or as to the conduct of a captain, or leader, or member of a patrol.

11th. By whoever shall be found gambling with any slave, or slaves, at any kind of gambling.

Art. 17th. It shall be the duty of the Parish Constable to receive and deliver personally to the person to whom they may be addressed all commissions, orders, notices or commissions issued by the Parish Superintendent of Roads and Patrol, relative to the patrol, without delay, and take receipts when necessary, and make returns of all services by him made to the said Superintendent.

Art. 18th. That all fines and forfeitures imposed by this Ordinance shall be prosecuted and recovered on information before any Justice of the Peace in this Parish, in the name of the Parish of St. Landry, for the use of said Parish, and shall be paid into the

Treasury of the Parish and applied as the other funds thereof: Provided, That the Justice of the Peace, before whom any matter arising under the provisions of this ordinance may be tried, shall judge of the sufficiency or insufficiency of any excuse that may be offered by any delinquent brought or cited before him, and shall give judgment accordingly.

Art. 19th. That the Parish Superintendent shall have the power to cause to assemble the whole Patrol of the Parish as often as he may think proper, at such place or places as he may designate, either on foot or on horseback and with or without arms. It shall also be his duty to designate to each patrol in each beat a place of rendezvous to rally in case of emergency.

Art. 20th. That the Superintendent of Patrols is hereby authorized to purchase powder, balls, and caps if necessary to carry out the objects of these ordinances.

Art. 21st. That all Ordinances, Resolutions and Orders of this Jury, heretofore passed on the subject of patrol, and conflicting with the provisions of this Ordinance, be and they are hereby repealed.

Ordained October 29th, 1862.

ELBERT GANTT, President. Jos. D. Richard, Clerk.